SO YOU WAN

BY DR. STEVE LUNT

Published by Starry Night Publishing.Com

Rochester, New York

Copyright 2017 Steve Lunt

Dr. Steve Lunt

Contents

Dr. Steve Lunt

FOREWORD

At the outset, let me indicate that I am a great advocate of sports in the schools of Utah and a great admirer of those in the coaching profession. In my more than forty years in higher education, I have met some very impressive educators, but I can honestly say at the very top were some of the coaches I have known. They were men and women who were exceptional teachers, in the finest and purest use of that word. They were not always successful coaches, though the majority of them were. They were people who made a significant impact on the lives of the athletes who played for them and for many of us on the sidelines as well.

One of the best was a basketball coach at the small rural high school I attended in the late 1940s. I suspect the coach did not know much about the sport of basketball, and he only lasted one year. He had been a varsity swimmer in college and was assigned the basketball coaching honors because there was no one else to do it. I remember seeing him come out of the old post office on Main Street, a very excited man. His book had just arrived from Quaker Oats: "How to Play Winning Basketball." Needless to say, our high school didn't win many games that year but the coach was a winner in every other way.

His players idolized him for the classy man that he was every player on the team wanted to be just like him. Even with his losing record, no doubt he would have been asked to coach the team a second year because the players and their parents would have demanded it. But the coach elected to go to California to get an advanced degree in education and, I'm told, rose through the ranks to become president of a large Los Angeles college.

So our town only had him for a single year, and that was too bad because he had been a significant motivating force in the lives of all who came in contact with him. He was smart and carefully attuned to the psyche of young teenagers. And all of them wanted to be just like him. They wore what they saw he wore, read the books he read, and, if they could have afforded it, they'd have bought a Chevrolet just like the one he drove.

He won the allegiance of his athletes by being their friend, by trying to direct them into lives of consequence and worth, by sticking up for them when others would not, by his unwillingness to compromise values for expediency, and by ensuring that everyone who wanted to be involved in his basketball program were. If he saw a student who was on the fringes of the student body and seemed friendless, he gave them an assignment with his team, running errands or sweeping the floors, anything to give the student a sense of personal worth. As I look back on the great teachers I have known, I'd put that basketball coach up there with the best of them.

It is too bad that he didn't have a copy of this small book on coaching prepared by Dr. Steve Lunt. Perhaps if he had had this book, the team results of his year in basketball would no doubt be glossier. Because if anyone knows the nuts and bolts of coaching, it is Steve Lunt, who was involved in teaching and coaching at Southern Utah University for nearly forty years. He has been an assistant basketball coach, an assistant baseball coach, head track and cross-country coach, and head athletic trainer. He served SUU as athletic director for nearly a decade, and was chair of the Physical education from 1979-. When I served as president of Southern Utah University, I asked him to take on the additional assignment of assistant to the president for special projects where he created campus opportunities in which upwards of 80 high schools participated in sporting events at SUU in a single year. In 1994 he was selected to receive the Circle of Fame Award from the Utah High School Activities Association, the only college or university faculty member to be so honored to that date.

The Southern Utah University physical education department has become widely known as "The Coaching Factory" for the number and quality of its graduates who have entered the coaching ranks. Their successes as coaches and teachers has earned the department, and especially Dr. Lunt, many accolades. I can truthfully say that in my years as president of SUU, I received more complimentary letters about Dr. Lunt than all the other faculty combined. The letters came from current students fortunate enough to be enrolled in one of his classes, from alumni, principals, superintendents, and parents of students.

He has been a master teacher and this book reflects some of the guiding principles he has gleaned in a lifetime in the coaching and physical education ranks. He has distilled the principles down to this small; very readable book which I am confident will be read and reread by its owners. It serves as a handbook in the art of coaching, and, of course, in the art of teaching too.

Gerald R. Sherratt
SOUTHERN UTAH UNIVERSITY (SUU)
President, 1981 – 1996

Dr. Steve Lunt

PREFACE

Those persons who desire to get into coaching an athletic team at any level, e.g. little league (youth sports), interscholastic, intercollegiate, intramural, extramural, recreation or professional, often times do not fully understand all that is involved in becoming a coach.

Often they aspire to coach because they once participated and still want to be actively involved in sports, or they have a deep desire to be involved even though they themselves may not have been an active participant or had a problem whereby they could not participate.

Having been a coach on the youth sports, interscholastic and intercollegiate levels, I experienced each of the the trials encountered with coaching. This included being the equipment manager, the athletic trainer (sports medicine), arranging transportation (including being a chauffeur), rooms, meals, ordering equipment and inventory control.

Currently being in the position of directing the preparation of those choosing to become a coach, and being responsible for the soliciting and hosting of a variety of sports events (dual-team, etc.) for league and conferences championships, as well as, high school state championships, I found that too often those pursuing coaching do not realize all that coaching entails.

This book is to help enlighten those who choose to get into coaching as to all the duties, responsibilities one will most likely encumber. To alert people of the many and varied tasks associated before they accept a coaching positions is the primary purpose of this book.

Coaching is not easy, if you want to be a good coach. Many people see coaching as a high profile glamorous position. The part of coaching most noticeable is about 10% of their job: show time and game time. What is not seen or known is the remaining 90% where all of the preparations and many problems occur.

Do not get into coaching for the wrong reasons. Pursue coaching with the attitude and intent required to be a good coach and role model. Society needs positive role models and leaders. This is the by-product of sports.

Dr. Charles Stephen "Steve" Lunt
SOUTHERN UTAH UNIVERSITY (SUU)
  Former Assistant to the President
  Former Chair, Physical Education Department
  Former Athletic Director
  Former Coach: Football, Basketball, Track & Field
  Former Referee/Official: Football, Basketball
  Former Head of Southern Utah Officials Association
  Organizer of "The SUU Coaching Factory"

CHAPTER 1 - WHAT IS A COACH?

"No power is strong enough to be lasting, if it labors under the weight of fear."

---Cicero

According to Webster, the word "coach" is defined as:

1) Person who teaches or trains athletic team(s); 2) a private teacher who helps students; 3) teach-train; 4) help prepare for a special test or event; 5) tutor.

To be a coach is one of the most encumbering professions there is. The exposure of sports in today's society is at an all-time high, so much so that some people (adults and youth) become obsessed.

The coach is the leader of a team, be it little league teams, interscholastic, intramural, city recreation, intercollegiate or professional teams. The needs and expectations for each team vary accordingly at each level.

A coach is held in high esteem by most people, but most importantly by their team. To these team members the coach is the ultimate, and they will do most anything the coach will ask or request of them, especially if there is admiration and respect.

In an interscholastic setting, the coach is known to and by nearly every student in the school. However, the coach will not know each and every student in the school.

Not only is the coach responsible for the team's conduct, appearance, sportsmanship, and behavior; but coaches are also accountable for liability situations with facilities, equipment, supplies, playing fields/court and the prevention, care and treatment of injuries sustained.

To be a coach you are "In Loco Parentis", which translates to "in the place of a parent." You are to treat and do for your athletes in much the same manner as parents would treat their child. As is often the case, some players can and have become more closely associated with their coach than with their parents.

To be a coach – to be a "good" coach – is different things to different people. You must be willing to do the best you can, to give your full interest, and effort so the team is not cheated or short-changed. Members of a team are there because they made the decision to become a vital member of an organization with a philosophy and goal with which they believe in and support. It is true, however, that some players might be there due to parental or peer pressure and is another aspect you must face.

I strongly feel there are some who should become head coaches. I also firmly believe there are some who should never become a head coach. The latter are more effective in an assistant or supportive role.

To be the head coach, you are the final authority. The buck stops with you in all the earlier aforementioned tasks. If you want to be a figure-head to accept all the glory and none of the responsibility, do yourself a favor, as well as, the players, parents, administration and fans: do not accept the role as head coach. The easiest part of coaching is _inside the lines_. The most consuming aspect is dealing with everything outside the lines. To be the type and quality of head coach people expect, you should dedicate yourself to all the facets, not merely the ones you choose to deal with.

This leadership role you assume is, without a doubt, one of the most stressful situations there is; dealing with each and every aspect. Yet, at the same time, there is nothing more rewarding than to conquer stress. However, this does not mean you have to win the championship or you are considered a failure. When all is said and done, there is only one champion in each sport; all others follow in order, but they should not be considered losers. If the coach and everyone associated have helped someone grow and develop, to become a better person than they were when the season began, then everyone is a winner.

To place winning above all else creates a false set of values and people act accordingly. Each year everyone should grow, learn and be better than they were last year; if not, they will not have an enjoyable time. They will learn to hate, just as much as they used to love, their participation.

What is a coach? It is a very demanding, high effective position. One that is necessary to be occupied; it takes a very special person to fill that position. Not everyone is capable to fill this position, just as not everyone can be a good mechanic, plumber, carpenter, or electrician.

Each position in life has its own special requirements, and some people are more qualified and better than others in fitting specific roles.

A coach is someone special, someone who leads, someone who is forthright, is honest and trustworthy, someone who is a role model because many eyes are focused upon the coach and they see things they never expected to see. In some instances, the coach is viewed (almost) as deity.

What is a coach? I ask, what doesn't a coach do or what aren't they responsible for? One thing about being a coach is that it has been and still is an addictive occupation for most coaches. To be a coach you belong to a great organization which has no yearly monetary dues, but you pay your "dues" in accepting all the rights and responsibilities that go with the position.

"If you think you are beaten, you are.

If you think you dare not, you don't!

If you want to win, but think you can't,

it's almost a cinch you won't.

If you think you'll lose, you've lost;

for out in the world we find success

begins with a fellow's will;

it's all in the state of mind.

Life's battles don't always go

to the stronger and faster man,

but sooner or later the man who wins

is the man who thinks he can."

--- Unknown

CHAPTER 2 - WHY DO YOU WANT TO BE A COACH?

"Lord, grant that I may always desire more than I may accomplish-"

--- Michelangelo

Most people who want to be a coach have usually been an active participant in a sport and found they liked the arena. Their attitude toward coaching most likely came from an association they had with a coach or coaches, who helped fill a void or a need when the participant needed someone or something in life. The job of a coach is to give players a feeling of self-worth, to help them build self-confidence, to help them feel they are a vital and important part of the team, etc., to provide praise when individual success has transpired, to console, cuddle and nurture when they or their team has not achieved the success they had so desired and determined to get.

Many times people get into coaching for the wrong reason. Some have been highly successful while being a participant and feel the normal or natural thing to do is to follow-up their active career by becoming a coach. Others who were not highly successful as a participant, feel an inner urge that they have learned from their success or lack of success. They want to help others achieve, grow and develop, and be the best they can be.

Then, there are others who become a coach to live out a fantasy career they did not have, and feel they are now qualified to help others achieve something they were never able to do themselves for whatever reason. This is especially true in youth sports prior to the individuals' involvement with interscholastic competition, which is the beginning of the battle to win a state championship for their high school.

Often times, a parent becomes a coach of a youth team so they can coach their own child. This is done with good intent, but sometimes does not work out very successfully. If their intent is to coach their own child to guarantee the child will make the team and play, they then are into being a coach for the wrong reason. Often these parent-coaches have no formal training in all of the aspects they will encounter. They usually lack the full knowledge of the skills each participant will need to be coached on, or the psychological aspects in dealing with their own or other's children, happy and unhappy parents, game officiating, caring for injuries received, arranging for practice sites and times, and having all the needed equipment available to play under safe conditions.

Too many parent-coaches create peer pressure for their child by showing, or perceived showing, favoritism toward their child by overly demanding or overly criticizing/humiliating them, either in front of teammates and peers or at home in front of family members. Lest they forget, people need a positive environment to bring desired success. Continued negative comments will bring continued negative results. Often times the success factor is more present than the participation factor. In fact, sometimes children who do not have the interest or desire to participate are forced into participation. As a coach, how are you going to handle and deal with these individuals?

There are many who turn to coaching as a profession because they are so used to having been a participant in sports and may have been neglectful in preparing themselves for a life after participation. Some of these people will take a very honest approach to their choosing to be a coach, but there are others who see only one side, that being the glory, fun and satisfaction the winning championship coaches receive. They do not see the down side. One of the down sides to coaching is that, like anything else in life, success does not come without a lot of work and the many hours it takes. If you get into coaching to be there only for the game or day of competition, do not get into it. Coaching requires a great sacrifice from you, "The

Leader," for you are expected to be everywhere, do everything, and have all the answers.

The great or best athletes do not automatically become good or the best coaches. Why? One opinion is that those who are good achieved success with their inborn abilities, things came easy; therefore, they never had to learn basic skills from the beginning, they could perform the skill already. If you did not have to learn how to perform a basic skill – that you can do it – how, then, are you going to teach simple skills to your athletes, if you do not understand? Success in life comes from knowing and understanding the basic skills needed – no matter what your career choice is.

Children are born knowing very little; they must be taught. As they progress, they develop inherent basic skills when their body is capable of handling the skill or situation. Not all children grow and develop at the same pace. Some sit up alone earlier than others, some crawl earlier or later; the same with climbing stairs, or walking, talking, feeding themselves, and being ready to enter the first grade. Everyone has their own comfort zone – so to speak – as to when they do something. Some nine year olds are ready to compete against thirteen year olds, while some thirteen year olds are not ready to compete against someone of a lesser age. You, "The Coach" must decide when it is time to put the proper challenge to the proper participant so Success can prevail. A dramatic negative experience can be very destructive to some participants to come out of their so called "shell." At least, it will take a lot of success and positive experiences to create a happy outlook and pursue success in the domain that was not a pleasant experience.

Suppose that you, as a coach (head or assistant) are relieved of your coaching responsibilities, secure another coaching position, but then are relieved, again, of your coaching responsibilities? What will become of your attitude toward coaching?

The easiest part of coaching is inside the lines, during games, but that is where you spend the "least" amount of time as a coach. It is all the other responsibilities that take the bulk of your time. Coaching can be very time consuming if you want to be successful. The coach who prepares their team the best, for every situation that might arise, will most usually also be the victor. Those who prepare the least most usually are the losers. Yet, it is true, talent usually wins, but by not giving talented athletes basic skills, preparation skills, those athletes will not always be winners. Cohesive team play – well prepared – will overcome lack of talent much of the time, as opposed to a team with more talent which plays with disarray.

If you think coaching is easy and part-time, so will be your success. As noted by the English author – Samuel Johnson – "What is Easy is Seldom Excellent."

"He who criticizes is seldom forgiven;
He who encourages is seldom forgotten."

--Gail Kemp

CHAPTER 3 - NEED FOR A PHILOSOPHY

"Anyone who always says what he is thinking, isn't thinking."

---Al Batt

Webster defines philosophy as: 1) the study of the nature of knowledge and existence and the principles of moral and aesthetic value; 2) the philosophical teachings or principles of a man or group of men; 3) the general principles of a field of study; 4) wisdom or insight applied to life itself.

Before you accept the task and responsibilities of being a coach, you need to take a personal inventory of yourself, of what you are, of who you are, and what is it that makes you think you can be a coach. You need to write down your philosophy of whatever it is you are trying to accomplish as a coach. Is it for your self-esteem or ego, or is it to help others to achieve success, whatever success is to them, so they have a varied and full life. Not everyone sees things the same way or in the same light as you. Your attitude and way of doing things will be seen at every practice or contest. You will be observed, assessed and challenged in ways you never thought were possible by family, friends, associates, participants, supervisors, administrators, officials, radio/TV/newspaper personnel, as well as the general public. Will your philosophy cause you to be put in awkward, embarrassing and humbling positions?

For you to be the type and quality of coach you expect of yourself – to include what your supervisors, peers, participants, officials, parents, media, and general public perceive to be the reasons why you are "The Coach," – take careful note of the following entitled *CLASS*:

CLASS

Class never runs scared. It is sure-footed and confident. It can handle whatever comes along.

Class has a sense of humor. It knows that a good laugh is the best lubricant for oiling the machinery of human relations.

Class never makes excuses. It takes its lumps and learns from past mistakes.

Class knows that good manners are nothing more than a series of small, inconsequential sacrifices.

Class bespeaks of aristocracy that has nothing to do with ancestors or money.

Some wealthy "blue bloods" have no class, while some individuals who are struggling to make ends meet are loaded with it.

Class is real. It cannot be faked.

Class is comfortable in its own skin. It never puts on airs.

Class never tries to build itself up by tearing others down. Class is already up and need not strive to look better by making others look worse.

Class can walk with kings and keep its virtue and talk with crowds and keep the common touch. Everyone is comfortable with the person who has class because that person is comfortable with himself.

Yes, your philosophy is vital and very important to you because it will dictate the kind of person you are, how you work with participants and others, and it will give you direction in the planning you do with your team or squad. The personality your players exhibit during practice and competition will be a mirror image of how you conduct yourself. For all the responsibilities you accept, whether mentioned or not, when you pursue and accept a coaching position, none is more important than having someone tell you "thanks" for all you did to be a leader and role model who had a very large impact upon their life. True lessons and values were learned which helped them see and deal with life in reality. These lessons will help them with the struggles they have already faced and help them pursue and overcome obstacles they will meet in their lifetime.

"The pressure is on us by the nature of the job.
Performance relieves pressure."

--- Fisher

Dr. Steve Lunt

CHAPTER 4 - QUALITIES OF A COACH

"The way I see it, if you want the rainbow, you gotta put up with the rain."

--- Dolly Parton

The ten most powerful two-letter words are: "If it is to be, it is up to me." So, "Coach", what are the qualities required of you in your coaching position? If you think that because you were a good player that you will be a good coach, think again.

The easiest part of coaching is "inside-the-line." This is a show time for all the time and effort you and your team/squad have put in to prepare for your opponent. Of all the aspects you have to do as a coach, game time usually takes up about 10% of your time. It is in the other 90% where most coaches fail. Of all those who become a coach in any capacity (head, assistant, volunteer, etc.), it has been reported that the average coaching career will last 3.8 years. It is a fact, you will not coach forever.

If you were to be the person hiring or appointing a coach, what qualities would you be looking for? What attributes make a good coach?

If you are seeking a coaching position which requires a collegiate degree, this means you are qualified, on paper, but what do you know about your sport, really? What do you know about each and every aspect related to your sport? This is your program to run, the success or lack of success depends upon you. Remember that 10% of your coaching position is "show time", the remaining 90% is where you spend your time. If you fail in the 90%, you shall surely fail in the 10%.

What are some of the qualities that are not listed on your collegiate degree which are so very vital? There is not one definite set or list you can use to check off, but when you get to the hiring interview it becomes evident you have the qualifications or are lacking. If a question is asked of you about a particular item or phase of coaching and it does not fit within your philosophy, how would you answer? By: a) telling the person who asked the question what they want to hear so you secure the coaching position, or b) accurate and truthful to what you believe? If you answer only in a way to get the position then you have created a conflict. If the conflict is with your superior, you most likely will not succeed. You'll lose your job.

Qualities are different things to different people. Remember one thing, it is you who applied for the job! If you do not like the way things are done and you are going to change them, think twice. An old saying about hiring goes like this: "he who plays the fiddle calls the tune". If I, as Athletic Director or Superintendent, hire you and pay you, I will tell you what and how, you will not tell me.

Often coaches are telling others about how hard it is to get along with their superiors and how things are negative, nothing ever gets done, and that they get no support from the administration. Let me put this attitude into a different perspective. For simplification purposes, let's say that a hiring athletic director (AD) has responsibility for ten coaches. Each coach has, on average, ten coaching issues they direct back to the AD. That's 100 additional problems that have been saddled on him, leaving the AD with significantly less time for their other responsibilities.

To alleviate these problems and provide much needed leadership, I suggest that some of the qualities of a coach should come under the letters: **DBMP/BMAS**. The letters stand for: "**D**on't **B**ring **M**e **P**roblems / **B**ring **M**e **A**nswers or **S**olutions." Let us now go back to the interview setting and bring in the "ten problems per coach" reference. Your college degree says you are qualified. The interview is to determine the qualities you possess for a particular job. Are you going to add another ten problems, which the Athletic Director does not want or need? Or are you the possessor of many qualities so that you take away ten of the AD's problems? Which would you want to hire? Which are you?

Once on the job you will need to learn who does what in the scheme of things as they relate to your coaching assignment. There are at least two people you need to know about, because they run the school. With their support, you will succeed, regardless of your win/loss record. Without their support you will not last, even if you have undefeated teams. These two most vital people are the secretaries and the custodians. Befriend them, involve them, treat them with the greatest admiration and respect; perhaps give to them flowers, or a box of candy, a cap or a t-shirt, and, then tell them thanks! The secretary handles the calls, mail, schedules, etc.; the custodian handles the facilities/fields, sets things up, and cleans up after. These two people put in almost the same number of hours you will, which are many, if you are to be successful. What qualities do you have that they need or want?

A coach is different things to different people. To the participants you, as the coach, are the role model. You become not a part-time parent, but a surrogate parent. Participants come from homes with a variance of parent or guardian arrangements. Your role as a coach is to teach discipline and teamwork, and this means you must be willing to spend healthy segments of TIME in meaningful conversation and monitoring them on and off the forum of participation. With this in mind, let me quote Frank Outlaw who wrote:

Watch your thoughts; they become your words.

Watch your words; they become your actions.

Watch your actions; they become habits.

Watch your habits; they become character.

Watch your character; it becomes your destiny.

Glen Beere wrote, "The importance of the leadership role of a coach can never be overemphasized. Simply stated, coaches must be positive role models since they have the greatest impact on all involved. The assumed responsibility given to a coach is the most powerful influence in the lives of all those they coach. The coach must teach VALUES as the center of the target even though it includes a number of by-products such as skills, recognition, and scholarships but, the focus--the bull's eye--is spelled V-A-L-U-E-S. We are talking about values such as: sportsmanship, honesty, loyalty, teamwork, integrity, self-discipline and courage. Values, the center of the target, must be emphasized in each and every practice/meeting and In each and every contest. The coach is the teacher/leader responsible to model and instill values in the lives of all their participants."

When a coach accepts team members into a sport, the coach receives players who have decided to exercise their privilege to participate. There is no law which states everyone has a legal right to participate, so when the coach accepts them they need to remember the participants can quit at any time for any reason. Therefore, coaches must do all they can to keep each participant encouraged to remain a part of the team.

Dan Valentine, years ago, wrote a message of inspiration titled, "Treat Him Gently, World" and I would like to substitute the word "coach" for the word "world", and let you, as a coach, react accordingly.

"Treat Him Gently, Coach"

My young son starts school today....it's all going to be sort of strange and new to him for a while, and I wish you would sort of treat him gently. You see, up to now he's been king of the roost....he's been the boss of the backyard....his mother has always been near to soothe his wounds and repair his feelings. But now things are going to be different.

This morning, he's going to walk down the front steps, wave his hand, and start out on the great adventure....it is an adventure that will take him across continents, across oceans....an adventure that will include wars and tragedy and sorrow. To live his life in this world, will require <u>faith</u>, <u>love</u> and <u>courage</u>. So Coach, I wish you would look after him.....take him by the hand and teach him things he will have to know. But, do it as gently as you can. He will have to learn, I know, that all men are not just, that all men are not true. But teach him that for every scoundrel, there is a hero...that for every crooked politician, there is a great and dedicated leader....teach him that for every enemy, there is a friend.

Steer him away from envy if you can....and teach him the secret of quiet laughter.

In school, Coach, teach him it is far more honorable to fail than to cheat....teach him to have faith in his own ideas, even if everyone says that are wrong....teach him to be gentle with gently people and tough with tough people. Try to give my son the strength not to follow the crowd when everyone is getting on the bandwagon....teach him to listen to all men—but teach him to filter all he hears on a screen of truth and take just the good that siphons through.

Teach him, if you can, how to laugh when he's sad....teach him there is no shame in tears....teach him there can be glory in failure and despair in success.

Treat him gently, Coach, if you can, but don't coddle him. Because only the test of fire makes fine steel....let him have the patience to be brave.

Let him be no man's man....teach him always to have great faith in himself....because then he will always have faith in mankind.

This is quite an order, Coach, but see what you can do....he's such a nice little fellow, my son."

Coach, you are many things to many people, but you are also all things to some people.

What qualities do you have to be a coach?

Character is defined by what you are willing to do when the spotlight has been turned off, the applause has died down and no one is around to give you credit."

---Lance Albert

CHAPTER 5 - COACHING, KNOWLEDGE, PERSONALITY/DECORUM

"Speak when you are angry and you will make the best speech you will ever regret."

---*Ambrose Bierce*

The biggest phony a coach can ever be is when that coach tries to emulate someone whose personality is different from his or her own. The phony reproduction is ever present from the very beginning. People throughout the history of the world who were highly successful or great leaders, had great accomplishments performed within their own way or personality. Sure, they usually had an idol of someone or something to inspire them, but they did not copy or try to be something outside their true personality and comfort zone.

In the world of athletics, when something new is developed or initiated by a coach, many others copy and try to implement it into their scheme of things. Often times it does not work for them as successfully as it does for whomever developed it. If a new concept does not truly fit your philosophy of coaching, it most likely will not work. As an example, maybe your football team is a run oriented team and you are a quarterback who has a great throwing ability and can do great drop-back and throw skills. However, the coach's philosophy is a running game, and your skills as a running team quarterback are not so good. Now reverse the scenario, and you are a good running option quarterback, but the coach's philosophy is a passing game and your skills are not so good; there could be a conflict between you and the coach. Who is going to win?

If a coach tries to implement a system he knows little about, the players find out quickly that the coach lacks the total knowledge of the system, and player confidence rapidly decreases. But, if the coach knows and understands every aspect of the system, the coach can teach it and the players will more readily accept the system.

During Vince Lombardi's great years at Green Bay, he coached what he knew and he coached within his personality. He was a tough taskmaster. His players knew they had to toe-the-line, yet he did not over coach. He expected perfection, but he also let players own abilities be utilized to the maximum.

The same can be said about John Wooden during the great success he had with the UCLA basketball dynasty. Wooden coached what he knew, demanded perfection of basic skills, and let a player's talents win games. He coached within his philosophy of how the game should be played.

As earlier stated, the easiest part of coaching is "inside the lines;" this is show-time and is about 10% (maybe less) of your real work as a coach. The remaining 90% of your coaching job takes in everything "outside-the-lines." This includes your knowledge of each and every aspect of the game. You must know and practice continually each skill each position and teach it to each and every player. A skill left untaught will be the weak link in your game plan and if your opponents discover it, either by scouting your team or by accident while competing against your team, they will take advantage of it. Sure, it takes a lot of effort, but did you not seek and accept the coaching position you have? Then do not cheat the players and the programs by shortchanging them, the school, the city, the parents and the administration.

"Coach", the great became great because they worked at it by learning everything they could about whatever it is they were doing. Those who try to imitate without knowing the whole story of what made the great people or great coaches great are doomed to failure through ignorance. How many real and truly "great" people do you know personally? Have you sat down with them, visited with them to learn from them the vital keys to their success; or do you know only what you have heard or read about them? If with such a skimpy fund of knowledge you try to copy and emulate their greatness, you will look phony and out of place. Then, what does this do to the confidence level people have in you as a person and as a coach?

If you think coaching is easy, let me again quote Samuel Johnson (1709-1784), *"What is easy is seldom excellent."*

Let me use football as an example to illustrate how often losses occur because the coach lacks knowledge. His philosophy is narrow and he does not know how to coach a specific aspect of the game. In nearly 80% of all football games played at any level, the outcome is determined by some phase of the "kicking game." You say, "What? This can't be." But, it is true. If you lack a kicking game, there is a weakness your opponent will dwell upon; they either found your weakness by scouting or found it during the course of the game.

What are these aspects of the kicking game which determine the outcome 80% of the time? They include: 1) Kick-off and Kick-off Return, 2) Punt and Punt Return, and 3) Field Goals and Points-after-Touchdown. To break down these aspects further, let's look at a kick-off. Do you have someone who can kick the ball? How did they learn to kick? Was it from your coaching? (I assume you were a kicker so you know each skill it takes.) Kicking skills include where and how to place the ball on the kicking tee so you get the best kick possible; just exactly the spot of the ball the kicker's foot contacts the ball for maximum distance; how far the kicker must run prior to kicking the ball and a proper approach speed. Plus, I assume you have measured the kicker's leg strength and had him working on a strength training program. A short kick gives your opponent good field position; a long kick most likely will put your opponent in a worse field position. That is, if you have coached all the rules related to the kick-off and have no penalties, each assignment of the eleven players is designed to prevent a long kick-off return.

Now maybe you have done all the aforementioned, but how often and when did you practice this phase of the game? For 15 minutes the day before your initial game of the season? A few times the day before each game? Remember "Coach", if you do not prepare and practice this aspect, don't blame the loss on someone else, this is your program.

In one college football season during Virginia Tech's first two games, the Hokies blocked a punt against one team and an extra point against another team, giving them 50 blocked kicks in 104 games. The coach, whose team was on a 12 game winning streak, said, "It's the quickest way to win a game. It's for long yardage and changes momentum. It's always something that's been important to us."

"Coach", this is a very vital strategy as it relates to winning: a long run (return) by your team; a long run against your team; you block a kick; they block your kick; you have a bad snap; they have a bad snap; you make a long field goal; you make a short field goal. How many other positive and negative things can and will go wrong?

Let's look at kick-off return. Do you have the best players in the best position for them? Has each been taught exactly what his assignment is? Do players know what to do if it is an on-side kick, a short high kick, a deep high kick, or a squib kick? If a hard line-drive kick goes to one of your five up-front linemen (who usually never handle the ball during a game), do they know what you want them to do? "Coach", this is part of the 90% of our job "outside-the-lines."

What do you do about the remaining aspects of the kicking game? Is the long snapper taught how to hold-tilt-release so punter or holder receives the ball in proper position with proper speed so he can get the punt off or the ball spotted for the kicker? What are the rules of the game as they relate to each player's assignment during one of these types of plays? Have you coached/taught them? If not, here is another weakness in your coaching.

"Coach", do you know all the rules related to the kicking game? If not, why not? Most likely it is because you have not really studied the rules and know what is and what is not legal or the options available. Many coaches get so worried about offense and defense play that they forget to learn the rules and coach within the rules.

So You Want to Be a Coach!

One rule in National Federation (high school) and the NFL that most coaches do not know about or understand was utilized by Vince Lombardi while coaching the Green Bay Packers. This rule applies to options available to the receiving team after a "Fair-Catch" or an "Awarded Fair-Catch." The rule states a team can put the ball in play on the next play by a "snap" or "free-kick." Lombardi exercised the "free-kick" option against the then Baltimore Colts. Green Bay, down by a point late in the game, forced Baltimore to punt from their own end zone. Green Bay signaled for a "fair catch" and utilized the "free-kick" where they placed the ball on the tee (at the yard line where the fair catch was made) just like a "kick-off," with the same restrictions as a kick-off enforced. Paul Hornung kicked the ball through the goal post for a successful field goal, which allowed Green Bay to win the game on the final play of the game.

The point is, Vince Lombardi, being the great coach that he was, knew each and every aspect and rule of the game and utilized them to his advantage to win. Without this full knowledge of the football knowledge of the football rules, Green Bay would have lost.

Now that we have discussed the need for the coach to learn and know everything there is to know about each and every aspect of one's sport, the same knowledge and understanding applies to each and every sport.

The decorum you display at all time (in practice, in the classroom, during a contest, while out in the community) tells people more about you than all the words that can be written. You are what you are and don't try to be someone or something you are not. A false front becomes very evident, for everyone knows who the coach is and they see everything you do. When you accept your coaching assignment, you are expected by all to be a positive role model, at all times.

Your decorum or behavior is most evident during show-time, that time which is 10% of your position, but the one most everyone witnesses and remembers. For this, others will emulate you, so when you do something (or think about doing something), look in the mirror at yourself and reflect how it will look to everyone else. Will you look like a "fool" or will you look "forthright -- confident -- knowledgeable," like you know what is happening, you understand it, and accept the consequences?

If you are an animated and hollering coach, getting after your players continuously, they soon tune you out. They might hear you, but they do not listen to you. Imagine what it would be like and how you would feel if your supervisors did to you as you do to your players. If they let you know about each and every misdeed you do, would you not tune them out? The great coaches "coach hard" in the 90% part of their job.

From personal observations, most coach's decorum is witnessed during "show-time/game-time," and most of the decorum comes when dealing with officiating. Let us look at this aspect. Most coaches do not know all the rules of their sport. When you do not know all of the rules, how then can you coach within all the rules? Remember in football the "Fair Catch" rule.

During your practices each day, do you enforce the rules yourself or let the violations go and hope they do not happen in a game? Well guess what, they will happen in the game. When it occurs and the official observes the rules violation and enforces it, how do you react? If you know the rules, you can challenge the official when it comes to rules application, enforcement and interpretation; you have no ground when it comes to "judgment" calls. You see the play the way you want it to be and maybe not as it really was. The official has to see it from two aspects: 1) advantage/disadvantage and 2) safety. You see the play one-sided and when the official determines that what was done is not in agreement with you, what is your decorum? "Coach", have you ever made any wrong decisions within your program? Who noticed and how did you react?

The traditional, and probably the most popular and glorious, coaching opportunities are in secondary, collegiate and professional positions. However, there is also a need for coaches in little league, junior league, city recreation, club sports, intramurals, extramurals, plus other instances of organized teams or squads. In most situations the sport is there for the participants, but often some coaches feel the team is there for them, with many being untrained, unprepared and unskilled for being coaches.

Parents often get very close to their child's participation. All parents see what they want to see in the child's participation, and it is not necessarily reality. They are biased and very protective. Is this not normal human nature? So, you as coach must deal with not only the participant, but the parents, surrogate parents, guardians and relatives. To each of these people, their children are all good athletes and good sports. They often can do no wrong.

Your job as coach is to bring out the best in each person under your direction. They will be in all shapes and sizes; abilities and capabilities; competitors and non-competitors; happy and love to play or sad and feel insecure or intimidated; on time and willing to do anything or late and wanting to do nothing. Each creates an opportunity and has an impact upon someone's life which can be very positive or very negative. I would hope you would take the "positive" route as opposed to the "negative" route. A parent once wrote to an advice column to ask: "Is it wise to encourage mediocre talent, or might such encouraging create false hope for significant success in life?" The advice given in response to the question was, "I'm all for encouragement for everyone. Besides, just look around, plenty of successful people have mediocre talent!"

"A good example is more effective than good advice"

--- Rose L. Korotkin

Dr. Steve Lunt

CHAPTER 6 - WORKING WITH SUPERIORS

"When you ask from a stranger that which is of interest only to yourself, always enclose a stamp."

--- Abraham Lincoln

What is a superior? Webster defines it as: 1) one who is above another in rank, station or office, 2) one that surpasses another in quality or merit.

Who is your superior? If you do not know, you had better find out. Sometimes it is different people for different things, and you should know and understand who they are. Sometimes it is "line-of-authority," other times it is merely a position of "courtesy". One area I feel strongly about is that you should communicate; give all the available information and facts you can to your superiors. Let them know everything as it relates to your program. **Let Them Decide What Is Important For Themselves – Don't You Decide What You Feel Is Important To Them**.

"Coach", do you not want to know what everyone on or associated with your team or squad is doing? When a problem arises that you know nothing about beforehand, how do you react? The element of surprise usually is not very positive.

It is true that some individuals who accept coaching positions put themselves on a pedestal and feel they are the only one and everyone else will bow to each of their demands. If you put yourself on that pedestal, you most likely will fall at some point. When you begin to make demands, some of which are not in accordance with the policy or procedure of the organization for which you are coaching, you soon will find out you are not the boss. You choose the basis for what your working relationship will be with your superiors and that basis can be one of harmony or one of grief. Remember the letters: "**DBMP/BMAS**"

This where you set the tempo. Remember, the easiest part of coaching is inside the lines, which is about 10% of your job. The remaining 90% of your job deals in working with your superiors and colleagues.

This list of "90% responsibilities" is long and includes (but is not limited to) the following:

- ☑ Schedules
- ☑ Practice
- ☑ Games
- ☑ Contracts
- ☑ Eligibility Rosters
- ☑ Program Policies
- ☑ Physical Examinations
- ☑ Parental Consent Forms
- ☑ Health Insurance Provisions
- ☑ Securing Proper Playing Supplies and Equipment
- ☑ Maintaining Safe/Playable Field and Court Conditions
- ☑ On and Off-Field Support Personnel (Announcer, Timers, Scorekeepers, Referees)
- ☑ Training Room Access
- ☑ On-Site Professional Health Care Specialists
- ☑ Preparation of Facility for Practice and Games
- ☑ Program Rosters for Fans and Media
- ☑ Concessions
- ☑ Parking
- ☑ Security
- ☑ Travel Arrangements
- ☑ Restrooms

So You Want to Be a Coach!

- ☑ Uniform Laundering
- ☑ Inventory Control
- ☑ Dealing with Each Athlete and Their Needs
- ☑ Working with Parents
- ☑ Fostering the Feeling of a Solid Home Life

Coaching is not easy, you have to work at it continually, but no matter what, you have to get along with and have the support of your superiors or you will not last. Even if you win <u>championships</u>, you can still be released from your much desired, much cherished, coaching position. Along with **DBMP/BMAS**, remember that if you and each of your subordinates create ten problems per day that your superiors must resolve, you most likely will not last. You will be one of the statistics of coaching: An average of 3.8 years!

Working with superiors may be cumbersome at times, but always remember, they are your superiors. Keep them informed with each aspect of your job, let them decide what is important for them to know. When you are in doubt about any aspect of your job or responsibilities, ask for guidance, don't assume. A little time in communication will save a lot of valuable time in trying to rectify, cover-up, or redeem something that has gone wrong. "Coach", you will not win all the battles, but if you have the support of your superiors you will win the necessary battles. Someday, sometime, somehow, and somewhere, "Coach", you are likely to be listed as part of a law suit; plan on it. When some of the aforementioned task or responsibilities are not done or your superior is not informed, or you do not seek proper advice or information, you will be held accountable.

"The best cure for an old grudge is a bad memory."

--- Dan Weinbaum

Dr. Steve Lunt

CHAPTER 7 - WORKING WITH SUBORDINATES

"The easy way out of a difficulty is often the hardest to find."

--- Guy Belleranti

Sometimes your working relationship with your subordinates is more encumbering than your working relationship with your superiors. Your superiors are only as good or as strong as their weakest faculty or staff subordinates. The same can be said about you and your program. Your program can only be as strong as your weakest assistant or support subordinate.

To build a very strong and viable program, you must surround yourself with the most qualified and competent personnel you can find. This does not mean hiring your lifelong friends. It means you need to obtain the best you can find. Maybe some of your friends are exactly what you need. On the other hand, you should not hire someone totally unknown to you. Hire a qualified candidate that either you, or a person you deeply trust, has full confidence in.

Most problems with all areas of employment are personnel related. Some want a position, not a job. They want to get paid for each and everything they do. Their attitude is "no pay, no work" beyond what a "union-wage earner" is expected to do. In "yesteryear", when people accepted a job, they "did what had to be done, whatever it was and whenever it was due, no matter how long it took."

The individuals you hire who have aspirations of moving up the ladder, those who have been an assistant and want to pursue a head coaching position, will usually understand the work ethic required to become a head coach. Those who have no desire to rise within the ranks have found a comfort zone and do not want to be disturbed. They will do the minimum that is needed, but will not pursue anything that takes more time and effort; they are content.

When accepting a head coaching position, one will want to be able to bring in their own people to assist; this is only right. It is the head coach who will receive all the "heat" when things go wrong, not the assistants. Therefore, a head coach needs his or her own team to work with.

How will you go about selecting your assistants? Will you use the buddy system, seeking referrals from your friends, or are you willing to see what is available by having open applications to gauge interest? The latter is generally one of the hardest decisions you will ever make as a head coach. The toughest decision will be when you have to release a close friend or someone you personally hired.

After you have selected your staff or subordinates, how will you treat and coach them, for they are now your team and they will be doing more coaching than you. "Coach", now that you are in the head position, remember the ten times ten rule. If you have ten subordinates and each of these ten bring ten problems, you now must deal with 100 problems before you can get to your responsibilities. In most instances, you will have to teach or coach them just as you and your staff will have to coach the team. You coach your team of players to have success and reduce errors. The same holds true for your staff of subordinates. Therefore, you need to coach your staff with every detail you want them to do and understand.

Yesteryear's work force would usually receive instructions and follow them. Today's work force is often different. After receiving direction from you, they may not do it as you instructed or hoped for. Today's workers might question everything you do with the comment, "why?" They want a reason for everything and if the reason does not fit their philosophy, they will question, "why?" Your philosophies will be tested many times over.

"Coach", in working with subordinates, you will have to plan and prepare very well for every aspect as it relates to your program, to include the finite details. It is better to prepare for each and every task, leaving no stone unturned, than it is to focus only with the main tasks and hope the small and insignificant details do not arise. For if you don't prepare for the small tasks, they shall surely come forth.

To prepare and not use is usually a better approach than to not prepare and then run up against something for which you were not prepared.

The subordinates you work with will want some areas of responsibility delegated to them. With some significant aspects assigned to them they will feel better about their job and better about themselves. When you do delegate, do not continue looking over their shoulders to intimidate or critique everything they do. Teach them just exactly what it is you want them to do and how you want it done. Then get out of their way. If they do not perform to your expectations, you have an easier time of helping or releasing them. If you are of the opinion that "you can do it all yourself," or do it better than your assistants then do everybody a favor, do not hire anyone as an assistant. Do it all yourself!

Your assistants want to be treated with respect. Certainly, within any organization there will be times when not everyone will agree. Many will come with their own philosophy and their own way of doing things. Recognize this and allow them to have input into your entire scheme. Their ways might be different from yours, but if their way brings the results you seek then give them the credit and recognition. You can learn from them and sharing credit strengthens the team. In the end, how well your team plays often determines the winner; it's not always the team with the most talent. Utilize the best skill of each player and each subordinate.

Teach your subordinates so they, too, can pursue and elevate to a head coaching position if that is their desire. Help them grow, develop, and mature. If there is conflict among the staff, your team members will know and feel the tension. If they are thinking about this aspect, they will not perform at their top performance. Learn to keep your door open and listen to what athletes are "saying" as well as to what they are "not saying." Do the same with your staff.

It has to be a fun and enjoyable experience for everyone – the coach, the assistants, the players, the administration and the parents. If it is not fun and turmoil exists then you, "Coach", will most likely be up on the losing end.

"Coach", get the best help you can, teach them, give them responsibilities, give them direction, give them support, and move out of their way. Give them recognition, give them awards, and give them respect in its deepest sense.

"It's a good idea to make sure you're on firm ground before you put your foot down."

--- Sam Ewing

CHAPTER 8 - ASSOCIATION WITH THE ATHLETES

"The bigger the problem, the more victorious the solution."

--- Rose Korotkin

"Coach", the entire focus of your coaching responsibility is that of the athletes, for without them you have nothing. The only product from your coaching is, what you have done for those who gave of their precious time to play for you. If you are into coaching for any other reason or purpose, get out....now!

Many studies, surveys, and questionnaires have been completed to find out about sports: the players, coaches, administrators, schools and communities desires and direction. But it all comes down to what is best for the participants.

What do the participants expect? What do they like and dislike? From one study conducted years ago, the following was reported as to what athletes liked or expected from coaches:

- A coach should be able to talk to me on my level.

- I want to have confidence in their advice.

- A coach must be fair and consistent.

- A coach should be able to give me help with my problems.

- I want to look up to my coach. I don't want my coach to be my buddy.

- I want my coach to be a person that I can really respect.

- I appreciate that a coach gives a lot of their own time.

- I appreciate their encouragement to try harder and to do well.

- My coach is a good teacher of skills and techniques; we do more than just play the game.

- My coaches care for me. I feel they have feelings for me beyond just being a player on the team.

- My coach is a real human being.

- My coach is someone to lean on. Sometimes I need help.

- My coach is always behind me, even when things aren't going well.

- My coach has the knack of being able to help each one of us individually.

- My coach teaches a feeling of enjoying competition and enjoying a sport.

- My coach must have had fun and enjoyment in their school or college, and is now making it possible for me to have that same good experience.

Just as important are things athletes dislike about their coaches:

- A coach that is too aloof.

- A coach that wants to see how much I sweat.

- A coach that thinks their sport is supposed to occupy my whole life.

- A coach that holds practice three to four hours per day.

- A coach that will bend the rules to win.

- A coach that will overlook infractions by star players.

- A coach that tries to "brainwash" us. We don't have to be turned into monsters to play well.

- A coach that will cheat to win. When you cheat, no one wins.

- A coach that has favorites who get special treatment, and when they are out of line, nothing happens.

- A coach that tells players they performed very poorly.

- A coach that cuts players down in front of other students and adults, sometimes during the game.

- A coach that has no discipline.

- A coach that has a trophy for a brain.

- A coach that cares only about the pay and honor for the job and doesn't care about the players personally.

- A coach that is two-faced.

- A coach that has favorite judges or referees.

- A coach that criticizes officials, even when the officials are correct.

- A coach who, before the game starts, won't let us talk to our friends who are on the other team.

- A coach that doesn't seem to like other human beings.

- Coaches that knock their job. If they don't like coaching, they should get out.

- A coach that cuts practice short so that they can take care of personal items.

- Coaches who don't get along well and criticize each other in public or argue in front of players.

- A coach that thinks a loss makes them look bad.

- A coach that doesn't know how to handle their job and tries to fake it.

- A coach that overlooks smoking and drinking.

- A coach who says the season is not important, only the tournaments count.

Other shared concerns from students include:

- I am disappointed whenever I see a coach swearing at the players. It even happens at tournaments in front of everybody.

- I don't like a coach that permits the starting line-up to run up a big score to make them look good. It's embarrassing to the team.

- I dislike coaches who don't set an example of what sports are all about.

- I don't like a coach that cuts corners to win. One night the coach sent in a player get into a fight with the "star" player on the other team. Both players were ejected – it was unfortunate for all who attended and participated.

So You Want to Be a Coach!

"Coach", you have the biggest impact on those athletes with whom you work and associate more than anyone else in the setting you are coaching (city, recreation, interscholastic and intercollegiate). In some instances you are in fact "In Loco Parentis", in place of the parent. You will spend more time daily with your team than they will spend with their parents.

If you are involved with junior high or high school settings, you need to know that you will not know every student; but, every student will know the coach and their eyes see and observe everything you do. No matter where you go or what you do, some of those eyes will see you and record in their mind everything you do, be it right or wrong. So when you are in doubt or even question yourself about doing something, be sure it is something you want to be seen as and known by. It might save your job or it might also cost you your job. It will certainly influence young athletes and prospective athletes on what they feel is appropriate behavior.

"All problems of mankind are found in the head, not in the heart."

--- Merry Brown

Dr. Steve Lunt

CHAPTER 9 - RELATIONSHIP WITH PEERS/ASSOCIATES

"School ends. Education doesn't."

--- Bern Williams

There are few professional careers that can be as rewarding as that of the "coaching fraternity or organization." The success, happiness and pleasure you derive from coaching is often dictated by your association with your coaching peers. Your personality, demeanor, knowledge base, ethics, honesty, loyalty, judgment and decorum are all part of what kind of association you have with fellow coaches.

No matter what you do in life, be it for employment, for recreation, or for friendship, your total success will be determined by your peer evaluations. If you are a coach who <u>must</u> <u>win</u>, at all costs, there will be times when something you did to win will come back to haunt you. You can win the game, but you also lose respect if you exhibit a sense of false values.

These peers not only include your fellow coaches, it also includes those who help make your team complete. Assistant coaches, volunteer assistants, managers, trainers, health care specialists, officials, and administrative support personnel are all people who have a vested interest in your program. If these people do not have any interest in helping you succeed, how will you function? You cannot do this alone.

Your relationship with your coaching associates will be a vital part of your overall success. As you are aware, coaches are very competitive at all times. If your peers and associates cannot bear to be around you, despite team success and winning championships, you might win the game but will lose the reward. You see, everyone is focused on winning, but winning will often bring out resentment in the opposition. It is intimidating for teams who consistently fail to appreciate teams who win. It may be in their human nature to loathe and despise winners. Fortunately, for coaches and teams who set the example of good sportsmanship, they will always find opportunities to excel.

There have been many to have been considered great coaches. However, there have been far more considered the opposite. "Great" is defined as: "much beyond the average or ordinary; mighty; eminent-distinguished; remarkable in knowledge of or skill in something." How is greatness identified? By won/loss records, by the good deeds one does, by helping others to succeed, and by developing character and values in your participants?

Athletics is a world of "copying," and coaches often times share their knowledge, philosophy, and techniques with others who want to learn about the successes they have had. After listening to what a coach did to achieve success, those in attendance will take some part from what they heard or learned and incorporate it into their scheme of things. If you feel you know it all and have all the answers, you have stopped learning and your peers will isolate you. As the quote at the beginning of this chapter states, "School ends, Education doesn't." You should take this to heart. Try to learn something different each day and add it to your knowledge base.

In dealing with those who provide support for your program, do not be afraid to seek their help or ask their opinion. Maybe they know something you do not know about a team member, about an opponent or an aspect you might not have been aware of or felt was unimportant. Maybe it is not very important to you, but it is to them or they probably would not have said anything.

If you have good health care services, and professionals are able to assist you and your program, listen to them. Their training is of a higher level than yours, and their evaluations and suggestions for treatment should not go unheeded or overruled. Health care has come a long way, especially for youth activities and, in many situations, the head coach is also the trainer. When you accept this responsibility, you are also taking on people's physical welfare, and maybe their lives, into your own hands.

A health care specialist will do what is best for the care and safety of the individual; but coaches worry most often about winning rather than the safety of the participant. If you deviate from the health care advice, treatment and rehabilitation provided, you will isolate them from your vital list of support personnel.

Fellow coaches you compete against and those you associate with are all so very necessary in developing your professional and personal friends and relationships. Very few people get very far or are very successful in life and in their careers without having some sort of resource people upon whom they care, share, and work with.

One of the most important skills you will need to nurture, coddle, and develop is "people" skills. If you cannot get along with or enjoy people and work with people from most every facet of society, then do not go into coaching. Your ultimate success is dependent upon not only you, but upon all those others who are either directly or indirectly affiliated with your program personally or as a fan and supporter.

If you develop arrogance and feel you know it all…that you can do it all yourself then you, "Coach", shall fail. And, if you have individual problems, remember that <u>winning an argument isn't worth losing a friend.</u>

"The bigger the head, the smaller the heart."

--- James A. Brewer

CHAPTER 10 - AREAS OF RESPONSIBILITY AND ACCOUNTABILITY

"Always go for it, for it will never come to you on its own."

--- Richard C. Miller

"Coach", when you were provided with the opportunity to become a coach, there were certain items you probably were aware of which were things that go with the title Coach; but, there are so many other aspects that go hand-in-hand with the position.

If you are hired as a head coach, you must first consider the fact that you are now an administrator. You are the administrator for the total program under your direction – every detail and each facet. When you are hired, they entrust to you facilities, equipment, supplies, participants and a budget. Being a head coach means the "buck stops with you." You will be challenged from every angle there is. You will have to make some tough, hard decisions. If you cannot do this, then certainly do not seek the head coach position, because your immediate superiors do not want to deal with problems within your program.

I hope you have entwined in your mind the letters **"DBMP/BMAS"** (see pg. 24) for they now take on more meaning. If you cannot deal with each facet of your program, and many items are passed on to your superior for completing or resolving, why do they need or want you? You are the administrator, you are the boss, which means you must do the job or you may be asked to vacate the position.

The facilities used by your program will be only as good as you want them to be, or as good as you take care of them. Yes, there will be support personnel from the administration, but most often these people do not see your team's facility in the same light as you do. They will do the minimal tasks to clean, prepare and set up, but they will not see all your needs; therefore, you will need to help yourself to help them. If you show a "lack-of-concern" attitude or desire, the support personnel will most likely see and follow your example. There are two role personnel who essentially run the school where you coach, and if they do not like you, you will most likely not succeed. These two very key and vital persons are the secretaries and the custodians. They can be your greatest help and advocates.

Regarding specific practice and game equipment, you need to know what is "on-hand", having an "inventory" of everything. When it comes time to purchase new items, you will have far greater success in getting what you need for your program if you can detail how the need will result in success. Plan carefully as you will most likely receive less than what you requested. With supportive facts you can provide a stronger case for your request. With few or no facts, it will be easy to turn down your request. To complete an inventory and to properly prepare your budget request takes time if you are to present your case in such a way that it will gain the support it will need for approval. If you think you can sit down and properly complete a budget request in an hour or two, you had better not plan on obtaining much support or allocation. You will get exact return for the effort you put in preparation – just as you do in coaching your team.

When ordering specific items, you need to know everything there is to know about each and every item, for practice and for competition. The more you know the easier it will be if: 1) you have to bid items, or 2) you order direct from a sales representative.

Without full knowledge, you will not receive what you thought you would or you will receive less desirable substitutes. Obtaining bids and ordering must be done well in advance of its first date of use. The more lead time you can give your provider, the more likely you will receive it when needed. If you procrastinate and fail to properly prepare, you had better plan to fail. Your orders are generally not the top priority of the provider. It is usually is like a meat market where you pick-a-number and wait in line. Have you created a problem or have you been a problem solver?

In preparing for travel to your competitions for scouting your opponents or attending clinics or camps, you will need to prepare a schedule of all trips and provide a breakdown for all anticipated expenses for each trip. This will include, but is not limited to: mileage (cost per mile) with mode of transportation, lodging, meals, and miscellaneous costs per trip. Along with this, you should prepare and distribute an itinerary of the dates and times of departure, hotel name and phone number, and time of arrival back home. To keep your superiors and all others associated to your team informed, this will do much to relieve anxieties, and in case of an emergency, they know where to locate you. Parents and wives do not sleep well until all the sheep are in and accounted for. This type of communication will do wonders for developing support, as well as, communicating with all involved. It is better to provide too much information, than too little.

"Coach", you need to learn all you can about injuries and recovery because you most likely will be the first one on the spot to see what has occurred and begin to administer emergency care. You need to not only have knowledge of EMT—CPR, etc., but also need to know what items you have available in your first aid kit, how each is to be utilized, and what to do if you need something you do not have available. In most instances, you now become the "athletic trainer". Now that the injury has occurred, how do you continue to treat the athlete, what rehabilitation will be needed, and who has the final authority to say when an injured athlete may return to competition? In this instance, I hope you do not put winning above health and safety for, if you do, you shall surely be the big loser. In fact, it might be a life vs. death or another crippling situation. If ever you have doubts about the health and safety of a participant, do the wise thing, "No Play" rather than contribute to a catastrophe.

You will also have to order injury prevention and treatment items and know how to use each. Can you properly wrap and tape most every part of the body if it sustains an injury? Do you know proper techniques so appropriate support is provided? Will you do something to make the situation or injury worse?

"Coach", all of these aforementioned aspects come with the title Head Coach. Sure, you may delegate, but in the end it all comes back to you. Are you truly and really capable to deal with and handle all of this? "Coach", this is part of the 90% of your time outside the lines, yet it has such a large impact on "show time", or that 10% of your job when competition is on.

Now come the two areas where most coaches get into problem situations: financial accountability and participation eligibility. The financial problem arises when there is a lack of/no control in handling money. The best way to ensure not having money problems is to not handle money. If you are doing fund raising or selling team packets (jerseys), have all the money turned in to the secretary, and get and keep receipts – DON'T HANDLE CASH! If you do travel and collect receipts, don't wait, do the reimbursement paper work ASAP. Procrastination will cause you to lose receipts. You might even be tempted to forge some – be careful. For any athlete to be eligible to participate, someone must perform an eligibility check. To be properly eligible to participate requires much work, time and effort. Depending on the level of competition, the sponsoring organizations all have specific requirements. Some are: age, weight, grade in school, area where they reside, amateur vs. professional status, academic work, number of credits, grades/gpa, years of competition, and in some instances, marital status.

"Coach", for you to not create your own "Problems", you need to plan and prepare well in advance of tryouts and competitions to make certain you have all the required information. It must be validated by proper documentation, not hearsay, such as: "they told me they passed enough credits and they would not lie." My advice to you is, when you see the birth certificate and transcript of grades, you can make the proper judgments based upon fact not upon "someone said" information. It is very unpleasant and embarrassing to all involved when a player participates but is later discovered to be "Ineligible" and you have to forfeit contests. "Coach", you are the ultimate person who is responsible. It is your program, each and every aspect! The buck stops with you! It is your program. Face it, you messed up. To do things late and in a hurry usually brings unwanted and unneeded problems. **DBMP/BMAS**. Learn to live by this at all times, and you will succeed in games and in life.

"Why is someone else's business always easier to manage than our own?"

--- Al Batt

Dr. Steve Lunt

CHAPTER 11 - LEGAL AND ETHICAL RESPONSIBILITIES

"May all your troubles last as long as your New Year's resolutions."

--- Joey Adams

Legal: according to law, lawful, legitimate, enactment, precept, regulation, decree, order, sanction, authority, permitted, statutory, due process.

Ethical: having to do with standards of right and wrong, in accordance with formal or professional rules of right and wrong, system of conduct or behavior, duty, what ought to be done, moral obligation, obligatory, imperative, with a safe conscience, as in duty bound, on one's own responsibility, at one's own risk, rules of conduct.

It has been noted at various times that in your coaching career you can plan on being sued at least once, so be ready and plan accordingly.

Who can sue? Anyone, for anything, at any time, within the statute of limitations, and that will be determined when the suit is filed.

A few legal terms you need to be acquainted with:

- In Loco Parentis: In place of the parent.

- Tort: A wrongful act or an infringement of a right (other than under contract) leading to civil legal liability.

- Liability: Responsible for, being susceptible, being under obligation bound by law to pay.

- Negligence: Failure to act as a reasonably prudent and careful person, lack of proper care of attention, carelessness.

- Reasonable/Prudent: Planning carefully ahead of time, according to reason, sensible, not foolish, not asking too much, common sense.

- Arbitrary/Capricious: Based on one's own wishes, notions, not going by the law or rule, guided by one's fancy, not the normal/expected way, unreasonable notions.

- Procedure/Due Process: The right to be heard, to tell your story or version, following legal procedure.

Not only must you do things for the participant, you must also follow the legal aspects of those organizations which govern and sanction your sport or activity. This includes but is not limited to: Little League Baseball, National Federation of State High School Associations, the National Collegiate Athletic Association (NCAA), and the National Association of Intercollegiate Athletics (NAIA).

When you participate under the sanction of one of the above organizations, you or whomever you work for usually must make application to that organization to see membership. They will then assess your application and either accept or reject the membership application. If accepted, you agree to uphold and live by the rules and regulations as adopted by that organization. Failure to live and function within the rules and regulations will cause problems, for which the penalty can be minimal or major. Remember **DBMP/BMAS**.

You need to always understand that the membership your organization holds is voluntary and by choice. No one makes any team belong to any organization, it is strictly by choice. It is a privilege not a right to hold the membership. Misdeeds can cause sanctions, penalties, punishment and loss of membership. It is your responsibility, as coach, to have a knowledge of the governing organization's rules and regulations, policies, and procedures. If you disapprove or disagree with something and want to buck the system, you will, in all probability, lose. If there is something you want to change, then follow the "Due Process". There is always a proper procedure to initiate change. Find out what that is and follow it. The procedure now becomes like a hurdle race in track. You clear each hurdle in proper sequence, but if you try to circumvent or go around a hurdle, you will be disqualified. Sure, it takes time, but it will prevent problems, which can result in loss of job. You, "Coach", will never be bigger than the organization itself.

When coaches feel they can do as they please, when they want something and no one can tell them differently, they should read and fully understand what transpired in each of the following situations:

***   *A Chicago high school wrestling coach says, "Politics, not opponents, is the reason my team tumbled from national rankings." The team was 15 – 0, but failed to crack the Super 25 after three years of top-three finishes. A publisher of a wrestling magazine said, "The school has suffered a drop in talent because of graduations and has wrestled weaker opponents because other top schools are not willing to schedule the team."*

The coach says other Chicago area schools harbor resentment of his school's legal battle with the Illinois High School Association the year prior. The association cancelled the state tournament rather than allow the school to compete because some of its wrestlers had entered five tournaments, one more than the association's limit.

"It's all a political issue; some people just don't want us to succeed," said the coach. The school got a temporary restraining order that allowed it to compete in the tournament. The association was denied a hearing at the state appellate and supreme courts. An opponent coach said some schools might be refusing to wrestle the school because of what happened. A lot of schools felt that there

was injustice, because it seemed as if they were a private school, and they played by a different set of rules.

The coach admitted his team had lost some talent, it returned only four wrestlers from the previous season. The association said the school could compete in this year's tournament only if it qualified.

From the foregoing incident, why would a coach put their team and school in the position where it causes punishment for all the other schools in their district or region, as well as, their own wrestlers, when the state association cancels the state tournament? Why do some coaches feel they are above the rules and regulations and expect no penalty? One coach took success and honors away from so many athletes because he wanted the rule set aside for his team when all other schools abided by the rule.

When an exception to a rule is made, that exception now becomes the rule for all others. If you do not like the rules, follow the procedure to get them changed, but don't initiate your own rules.

***Seven High School players in Kentucky sued their principal and former coach because their 10 – 0 team was declared ineligible for the playoffs for using an ineligible player. The lawsuit accused the former football coach and principal for failing to adequately monitor the football program and intentionally allowing the seven players to participate on a team with an ineligible player. The seven players were starters. The lawsuit sought damages for psychological injuries, emotional distress and loss of college scholarship opportunities suffered by the players.*

"Coach", there are a lot of items that deal with being a coach and 90% of your time will be taken up by handling the aspects found outside the lines. The aforementioned situation pertains to one such aspect. It is your responsibility to verify the eligibility of each of your participants. Remember the **DBMP/BMAS** slogan. Your superiors in administration do not want or need problems from you, such as student and athlete eligibility.

****Contracts of the women's basketball coaches at a university have been renewed. They were the objects of a sexual harassment investigation. The contracts were renewed nine days after they had been told they would be fired.*

Four players quit the team the month prior, claiming they were sexually harassed by the two coaches. The players claimed the coaches spread rumors that they were lesbians. The executive for university relations who headed the investigation had said that both had been found innocent. But he recommended that both be fired because they violated university rules by not punishing two players, one for smoking marijuana and the other for shoplifting.

As a coach, your duties and responsibilities are unlimited. Not only must you win, and in most instances teach and/or have other employment responsibilities, you are expected to know about all things that occur with your team. You are to police everything, including yourself and your staff. These are the part of what happens outside-the-lines. This is more of the 90% of your coaching responsibilities no one notices until something goes wrong.

****A high school football team, ranked number one in the state, faced a possible forfeiture for using an ineligible player in a league game. The league principals were to decide how to penalize the league champions for playing a "sophomore" kicker in a 34 – 0 win. The kicker, who transferred from one school to another, was "eligible only" to play in sophomore and junior varsity games. He participated in only two plays where he kicked off following the third and fourth touchdowns. The principal said, "We will accept whatever actions need to take place," however he acknowledged, that the offense appeared "not blatant unless the principal found more information that makes it worse."*

No matter what the circumstance or setting in which you are a coach, it is your responsibility to "know and understand" the player eligibility. Ignorance is no excuse. To plead ignorant is vacating one of your most important responsibilities. Without eligible players you have no team. For you to <u>assume</u> your players are eligible is one of the biggest errors you can make. The biggest error, as it relates to eligibility, is to take a player's word that they are eligible. The player's transcript of academic records declares eligibility. You, or someone assigned to check player eligibility, merely "verify" eligibility status; the proper or legal paper work "determines" eligibility.

***A Florida high school charged with a plethora of recruiting violations, was stripped of its boys' basketball title and had to forfeit victories in basketball (36), baseball (27), and boys' soccer (21). This was the first time a Florida school had been stripped of a state championship since 1971. Not only was the school banned from state tournament competition in baseball and basketball for one year, it could not compete in out-of-state contests. In addition, eight athletes in three sports were declared ineligible for living out of the district or for falsifying addresses. Not only were they barred from competing at the school for the next season, but at any other Florida High School Athletic Association member school as well.*

The school was notified it was fined $2,550 and must reimburse the FHSAA the $5,155 it spent on the investigation. FHSAA Commissioner said, "It's hard for me to believe that the administration was not aware that this was occurring. This is one of the most, if not the most, blatant violations of FHSAA rules against recruiting that I have encountered in my years as commissioner. These were not violations of omission, but of commission, and could only have been allowed to occur; or continue to occur, through a lack of institutional control."

"Coach", you are ultimately responsible for each and every facet as it relates to to your program. To not be in total control and held responsible is like saying, "I don't look for it, therefore, I don't see it"; yet you know yourself what is transpiring. In your position, you are guilty by association. Now the burden is placed directly upon you. You have two choices:

1) Deny, or 2) admit, then do what is right and what ought to and needs to be done.

The legal, ethical and moral obligations placed upon you, as the head coach, should never be underestimated, taken lightly, passed over or ignored in any aspect. For if you shirk your duties, someday, sometime, somewhere when you least expect it, you will find yourself embroiled in conflict. Remember the long-time saying, *"an ounce of prevention, is worth a pound of cure,"* or better yet, *"identify everything that can go wrong and then prevent it from happening."*

Just imagine in the NASA space program everything that must occur, without failure and in proper sequence, in order to have a successful mission. To have man walk on the moon and return to earth without failure, it took nearly 1.5 million functions to successfully occur. To not have this same success, it takes only one element to malfunction to lead to failure.

"Coach', you are the commander, the chief, the boss, the top dog and everything in your program reverts back to you. You have to make that final decision. If you cannot assume all of what is required, then not pursue being a coach, at least not the head coach. Become an assistant and be the best assistant you can be. Help make the job of the head coach easier and less cumbersome, then everyone wins.

"Do something today that will be a pleasant memory in the future."

--- Bern Williams

Dr. Steve Lunt

CHAPTER 12 - RELATIONSHIP WITH THE MEDIA

"Your future depends on many things, but mostly on you."

--- The Furrow

For any program or event to be successful, it is imperative that you have a full understanding of your obligations to the media. You should do everything in your power to make the job of the media easier. With the help of the media you can survive and things will be better; but without the help of the media, your event will not be nearly so successful.

The biggest task in working with the media is really nothing more than COMMUNICATION. To help illustrate, how often do you find out about something after the fact? And what is your opinion or mood? Neither you nor anyone else likes to be caught off-guard, unaware or by total surprise. The normal reaction is negative in some sense or tone of voice.

The media are available to provide you with assistance so your event is successful and pleasurable. The media is entitled to its opinion about you, your program, and your event. Just as you have your opinion about the media.

For the media to better help and assist you, you need to be totally prepared with all the information they need and it has to be accurate. If you provide inaccurate or only partial information and it limits their capability, you most likely will fall out of favor and will have a hard time recovering. The media operate on deadlines, which at times may not be in sync with with your schedule. To avoid a conflict, you need to spend as much lead time in preparation of information as you do in getting ready for a season or event. The more lead time the media receives, the better they can establish their work loads. Most likely, you and your program will not be the only event the media will be covering.

To continue with the illustration, some items you need to be responsible for include: provide an accurate schedule of games and events, listing proper names of opponents, location of contest and time of contest (every year I have seen schedules of two opposing teams and the date, location and times differ); provide an accurate roster (both numerically and alphabetically, this helps for a quick identification) giving proper uniform number and position, height, weight, and year in school; compile personal statistics, background profile of honors, award, leadership positions and have everything readily available should the media request it.

Be honest with information; i.e. if someone is not going to participate, let the media know so they can properly prepare. Maybe an injury to a special player will generate more interest in your program. This could be highly positive to see how you adjust and prepare your team with a vital participant missing. Do not expect favors in return for no favor given.

Dealing with the hometown media is pretty easy because they can get information more easily. Out-of-town or state distributed newspaper or TV usually have little, if any, information readily available about your team, unless you have the top program in your district, region or state (everybody follows the winners). Make certain they have accurate schedules so information printed or released by them is accurate. If a game time changes, be sure to inform the media, don't let them get caught off guard. If the media is not in attendance at your contest, be sure you or someone you designate reports the results with support information and statistics. Don't be one of those who calls when you win, but never calls when you lose. This creates the sour-grapes reputation with them and they lose trust in you.

An example of the aforementioned reliability, I read the following from a state-wide circulated newspaper: "Speaking of game reports, Kudos to the football coach who reported every name and scoring play of his team's 56 – 18 loss on Friday night although his team was the only team going into last week's action that had already been eliminated from the playoffs. Now that's class."

Don't you be the judge of what is important to the media; don't you decide what is and is not necessary. Provide the media with everything you can. The more information they have, the easier it is to report. How do you feel when someone only tells you what they feel is necessary for you to know?

Yes, at times the media can be disturbing and disruptive, but they are only doing their job, trying to assist you and your program. You need them just as much, if not more, than they need you. They always have something to do, writing and reporting. It is you and your program which needs exposure and the reporting of your success or lack thereof.

Communicate, communicate, communicate are three very important words you need to adhere to; do it when it needs to be done, and with full accuracy.

"The only thing that comes without hard work is unemployment."

--- Al Batt

Dr. Steve Lunt

CHAPTER 13 - FOOD FOR THOUGHT

"The person who smiles when everything goes wrong has already thought of someone he can blame it on."

--- Laura Namath

Throughout your entire life you will encounter many successes and failures. This is the way it has been and shall always be. As a coach you will not win each and every game. We all learn from our failures and mistakes, if we try. You need to realize that nearly everyone wants to win or to be a winner. At the same time many people hate the winner. This can be termed jealousy, envy, spite, malice or covetousness. The fact of the matter is everyone wants to beat the winner. In the end, when all is said and done, there is only one winner. All others finished with a loss.

Your attitude toward winning and losing will have a direct effect upon all those you coach or associate with. If you win but demonstrate an egotistical attitude, others will be turned off. If you lose yet still hold your head high and elevate others to not dwell on a loss, you will be a WINNER. You will never be bigger than life, but your attitude can either make it miserable for some, or uplifting and inspiring for many. It's up to you!

****

"Failure is not falling down, but rather not getting up."

--- Anonymous

****

EXCELLENCE

Excellence is never an accident. It is achieved in an organization or institution only as a result of an unrelenting and vigorous insistence on the highest standards of performance. It requires an unswerving expectancy of quality from the staff and volunteers.

Excellence is contagious. It infects and affects everyone in the organization. It charts the direction of the program. It establishes the criteria for planning. It provides zest and vitality to the organization. Once achieved, excellence permeates every aspect of the life of the organization.

Excellence demands commitment and a tenacious dedication from the leadership of the organization. Once it is accepted and expected, it must be nourished and continually reviewed and renewed. It is a never-ending process of learning and growing. It requires a spirit of motivation and boundless energy. It is always the result of a creatively conceived and precisely planned effort.

Excellence inspires; it electrifies. It impacts every phase of the organization's life. It unleashes an impact which influences every program, every activity, every committee, and every staff person. To instill this in an organization is difficult; to sustain it is even more challenging. It demands adaptability, imagination and vigor. But most of all, it requires from the leadership a constant state of self-discovery and discipline.

Excellence is an organization's life-line. It is the most compelling answer to apathy and inertia. It energizes a stimulating and pulsating force. Once it becomes the expected standard of performance, it develops a fiercely driving and motivating philosophy of operation. Excellence is a state of mind put into action. It is a road-map to success. When a climate of excellence exists, all things – staff work, volunteer leadership, finances, and programs – come easier.

Excellence in an organization is important because it is everything.

****

"Success is peace of mind which is a direct result of self-satisfaction in knowing you did your best to become the best that you are capable of becoming."

--- John R. Wooden

****

"He is best educated who is most useful."

--- Anonymous

****

DON'T BE AFRAID TO FAIL

Athletes, like all people, fall into two motivational classes: those who truly want success and those who simply try to avoid failure. Those who want success are the highly competitive leader types. They perform better under pressure; they thrive on it. The athlete who just doesn't want to look bad is not truly concerned deep-down about winning. If he competes with someone who is just as good, or better than he is, he often panics and blows it.

One of the quickest ways to become a loser is to want to win so badly that you are afraid to lose. When that happens, you start hitting your irons to avoid the traps instead of going for the flag; you throw the pass away from the defender to avoid being intercepted, rather than to the receiver. You tense up, you push, and you lose.

If you have prepared correctly, you should go into a game having every reason to expect you will win. But should you not, pick up the pieces and start again tomorrow.

No matter what the score, you'll never be a loser if you always look at an athletic contest as an opportunity to discover some weakness in your game that needs to be corrected. Don't be afraid to seek out tough competition, because then you will be tested to your limit and you can find out where your problem areas are.

You'll be remembered for the times you win, not the times you lose. Babe Ruth is a legend because he was baseball's Home Run king; he was also baseball's Strikeout king. People remember his home runs but not his strikeouts.

Jack Nicklaus and Arnold Palmer are two of golfing's greats, but they didn't win every tournament they entered.

There is a big difference between being concerned about winning or losing and being concerned about making the effort to win. When you're concerned only about winning, you're worrying about something that you can't completely control. When you are emotionally attached to results that you can't control, you tend to become anxious and try too hard. You can only control the effort you put into winning.

Don't use up your energy worrying about losing. Put that energy toward the effort needed to win. Valor grows by daring, fear by holding back. "Dare and you might; hold back and you never will."

* *

"A highly motivated team is a team that has been very soundly prepared. If you want to be Champions, you've got to perform like Champions every week."

--- Tom Osborne

* *

So You Want to Be a Coach!

J.C. Penney's

"SECRET OF SUCCESS"

"For every man there is a spark which, if kindled, will set the whole being afire until he becomes a human dynamo capable of accomplishing almost anything to which he aspires.

Too many people want to succeed, but will not pay the price of success.

Some folks have a wishbone instead of a backbone. They are not willing to subject themselves to hard labor. They can see easily enough how the law of cause and effect must work out for other people, but they expect to have it suspended for them.

Too many people think about pull, when they should think about push. They believe in luck, not pluck."

****

"Keeping the momentum going means you have to keep up with the motivation, the details. You've got to keep bearing down because once you're up there, there's only one place you can go.....down."

--- Bill Foster

****

"There's a winner in every game or it's not a game. Even debating teams try to win. When they start putting the loser on top of the winner, losing is what I'll strive for."

--- Earl Weaver

****

"THE MAN WHO THINKS HE CAN"

If you think you are beaten, you are;

If you think you dare not, you don't.

If you like to win, but think you can't,

It's almost a cinch you won't.

If you think you'll lose, you're lost.

For out in the world we find

Success begins with a fellow's will;

It's all in the state of mind.

If you think you are outclassed, you are;

You've got to think high to rise.

You've got to be sure of yourself before

You can ever win a prize.

Life's battles don't always go

To the stronger or faster man;

But soon or late the man who wins,

Is the man who thinks he can.

--- Walter D. Wintle

EXTRA EFFORT

There is no doubt that Vince Lombardi was right when he said, "Fundamentals win it." But sometimes, both teams may be fundamentally sound and you will need more to win. Once in a while you're going to have to reach down deep for that something extra. Some call it adrenalin, some call it second effort. Call it what you will, the great athletes have it.

The reason the great athletes have it is because they want to win so badly. Every time they step on the court or walk onto the field, they have made up their minds that they will do whatever is needed to win. If doing their best isn't going to do it, they'll do more. They'll make that extra effort to win. They do today what they have to do today. They worry about tomorrow, tomorrow. In short, they're winners and they do what is necessary to do to win, that's what extra effort is all about.

It's important to know exactly what that extra effort is and when to use it. Many athletes have lost not because of a lack of effort, but because of too great an effort, trying too hard instead of playing with relaxed concentration.

Extra effort means different things in different sports. In highly skilled sports like tennis, gymnastics, bowling, or even hitting a baseball, the extra effort means a deeper concentration and complete self-control. By trying too hard, you will lose your rhythm or tempo.

In other, more physical sports, such as wrestling, boxing, blocking and tackling in football, or rebounding in basketball, you don't have to worry quite so much about tempo. You can go a little, "like George Brett", berserk. Still, though, you must maintain your self-control.

Sometimes this extra effort comes down to conditioning. When two players or two teams are evenly matched, the one in the best condition usually comes out the winner.

Another athlete may be running 30 minutes after practice. Run 33 minutes and run hard. Get your edge, you may need it.

****

"A leader is a person with a magnet in his heart and a compass in his head."

--- Anon.

****

This definition tells us that the leader is going in the right direction and taking people with him.

****

"We play with enthusiasm and recklessness. We aren't afraid to lose. If we win, great. But win or lose, it is competition that gives us pleasure."

--- Joe Paterno

****

COACHES NEVER LOSE

A team can lose. Any team can lose. But in a sense, a very real sense, a coach never loses. For the job of a coach is over and finished once the starting whistle blows. He knows he's won or lost before play starts.

A coach has two tasks. The first task is to teach skills: to teach an athlete how to run faster, hit harder, block better, kick farther, and jump higher.

The second and major task, is to make men and women out of boys and girls.

The coach's purpose is to teach an attitude of mind. It's to implant character and not simply to impart skills.

It's to teach athletes to play fair. It's to teach them to be humble in victory and proud in defeat. This goes without saying.

More importantly it's to teach them to live up to their potential no matter what that potential is.

It's to teach them to do their best and never be satisfied with what they are but to strive to be as good as they could be if they tried harder.

A coach can never make a great player out of a boy or girl who isn't potentially great. But he can make a great competitor out of any child. And, miraculously, he can make a man out of a boy or a woman out of a girl.

For a coach, the final score doesn't read so many points for my team, so many points for theirs. Instead it reads: so many men or women out of so many boys or girls.

And this is a score that is never published. This is the score they read to themselves and in which they find their real joy when the last game is over.

****

"Fear of failure is a powerful obstacle to overcome. Sometimes we must realize that your best may just not be good enough."

--- Reggie Jackson

****

"I can't stand a ballplayer who plays in fear. Any fellow who has a good shot has got to take it and keep taking it. So he misses – so what?"

--- Red Auerback

****

"No one can make you feel inferior without your consent."

--- Eleanor Roosevelt

****

"If you want something to happen,

You have to make it happen.

If you wait for it to happen,

What happens is not what you want to happen."

--- Dr. Steve Lunt

<u>Starry Night Publishing</u>

Everyone has a story...

Don't spend your life trying to get published! Don't tolerate rejection! Don't do all the work and allow the publishing companies reap the rewards!

Millions of independent authors like you, are making money, publishing their stories now. Our technological know-how will take the headaches out of getting published. Let "Starry Night Publishing.Com" take care of the hard parts, so you can focus on writing. You simply send us your Word Document and we do the rest. It really is that simple!

The big companies want to publish only "celebrity authors," not the average book-writer. It's almost impossible for first-time authors to get published today. This has led many authors to go the self-publishing route. Until recently, this was considered "vanity-publishing." You spent large sums of your money, to get twenty copies of your book, to give to relatives at Christmas, just so you could see your name on the cover. Now, however, the self-publishing industry allows authors to get published in a timely fashion, retain the rights to your work, keeping up to ninety-percent of your royalties, instead of the traditional five-percent.

We've opened up the gates, allowing you inside the world of publishing. While others charge you as much as fifteen-thousand dollars for a publishing package, we charge less than five-hundred dollars to cover copyright, ISBN, and distribution costs. Do you really want to spend all your time formatting, converting, designing a cover, and then promoting your book, because no one else will?

Our editors are professionals, able to create a top-notch book that you will be proud of. Becoming a published author is supposed to be fun, not a hassle.

At Starry Night Publishing, you submit your work, we create a professional-looking cover, a table of contents, compile your text and images into the appropriate format, convert your files for eReaders, take care of copyright information, assign an ISBN, allow you to keep one-hundred-percent of your rights, distribute your story worldwide on Amazon, Barnes & Noble and many other retailers, and write you a check for your royalties. There are no other hidden fees involved! You don't pay extra for a cover, or to keep your book in print. We promise! Everything is included! You even get a free copy of your book and unlimited half-price copies.

In four short years, we've published more than fifteen-hundred books, compared to the major publishing houses which only add an average of six new titles per year. We will publish your fiction, or non-fiction books about anything, and look forward to reading your stories and sharing them with the world.

We sincerely hope that you will join the growing Starry Night Publishing family, become a published author and gain the world-wide exposure that you deserve. You deserve to succeed. Success comes to those who make opportunities happen, not those who wait for opportunities to happen. You just have to try. Thanks for joining us on our journey.

<u>www.starrynightpublishing.com</u>

<u>www.facebook.com/starrynightpublishing/</u>

Made in the USA
Columbia, SC
02 February 2023

11450186R00048